With a very best wishes
for Anne and David
great practitioners
of love

Margaret + Henk

August 30, 2006

from the Heart

from the Heart

A Collection of Vows, Blessings, and Wishes

**Andrews McMeel
Publishing**

Kansas City

FROM THE HEART

Copyright © by Elwin Street Ltd 2005
For information, write Andrews McMeel Publishing, an Andrews McMeel Universal
company, 4520 Main Street, Kansas City, Missouri 64111.

Conceived and produced by
Elwin St Ltd
79 St John St
London EC1M 4NR
www.elwinstreet.com

ISBN-13: 978-0-7407-5457-9
ISBN-10: 0-7407-5457-2
Library of Congress Control Number: 2005921770

Illustrations by Tracy Walker
Designed by Maura Fadden Rosenthal

Permissions
p36 – From Best of Chief Dan George by Chief Dan George and Helmut Hirnschall,
published by hancockhouse.com

Every effort has been made to obtain permissions for material used in this book and
to contact the copyright holders. The publishers apologize for any omissions and
would welcome contact from copyright holders for correction in subsequent editions.

PRINTED IN CHINA
05 06 07 08 09 TOP 10 9 8 7 6 5 4 3 2 1

CONTENTS

I'll write no love letter

I'll write no love letter and no poem—I'll just send a white kerchief to tell you my thoughts. When you receive it, look at it this way and that: The warp is all threads, and the weft is all threads. Who will understand what is in my heart?

A Vow to
Heavenly Venus

We that with like hearts love, we lovers twain,

New wedded in the village by thy fane,

Lady of all chaste love, to thee it is

We bring these amaranths, these white lilies,

A sign, and sacrifice; may Love, we pray,

Like amaranthine flowers, feel no decay;

Like these cool lilies may our loves remain,

Perfect and pure, and know not any stain;

And be our hearts, from this thy holy hour,

Bound each to each, like flower to wedded flower.

My sweetheart's dainty lips

My sweetheart's dainty lips are red,
With ruby's crimson overspread;
Her teeth are like a string of pearls;
Down her neck her clustering curls
In ebony hue vie with the night,
And over her features dances light.

The twinkling stars enthroned above
Are sisters to my dearest love.
We men should count it joy complete
To lay our service at her feet.
But oh what rapture is her kiss!
A forecast 'tis of heavenly bliss!

YEHUDAH HA-LEVI
(c. 1080–1141), Spanish, Jewish poet

In the future

In the future, happy occasions will come as surely as the morning. Difficult times will come as surely as the night. When things go joyously, meditate according to the Buddhist tradition. When things go badly, meditate. Meditation in the manner of the Compassionate Buddha will guide your life.

To say the words love and compassion is easy. But to accept that love and compassion are built upon patience and perseverance is not easy.

Celtic vow

You cannot possess me for I belong to myself

But while we both wish it, I give you that which is mine to give

You cannot command me, for I am a free person

But I shall serve you in those ways you require and the honeycomb
will taste sweeter coming from my hand

I pledge to you that yours will be the name I cry aloud in the night
and the eyes into which I smile in the morning

I pledge to you the first bite of my meat and the first drink from
my cup

I pledge to you my living and my dying, each equally in your care

I shall be a shield for your back and you for mine

I shall not slander you, nor you me

I shall honor you above all others, and when we quarrel we shall do
so in private and tell no strangers our grievances

This is my wedding vow to you

This is the marriage of equals.

Love is patient, love is kind

Love is patient, love is kind. It does not envy, it does not boast, it is not proud. It is not rude, it is not self-seeking, it is not easily angered, it keeps no record of wrongs. Love does not delight in evil but rejoices with the truth. It always protects, always trusts, always hopes, always perseveres.

When two people are at one

When two people are at one
in their inmost hearts,
they shatter even the strength of iron or bronze.
And when two people understand each other
in their inmost hearts,
their words are sweet and strong,
like the fragrance of orchids.

FROM THE I CHING

You are my husband

You are my husband

My feet shall run because of you

My feet dance because of you

My heart shall beat because of you

My eyes see because of you

My mind thinks because of you

And I shall love because of you.

TRADITIONAL INUIT LOVE POEM

Now you will feel no rain

Now you will feel no rain, for each of you will be shelter for the other. Now you will feel no cold, for each of you will be warmth to the other. Now there will be no loneliness, for each of you will be companion to the other. Now you are two persons, but there is only one life before you. May beauty surround you both in the journey ahead and through all the years. May happiness be your companion and your days together be good and long upon the earth.

Love one another

Love one another, but make not a bond of that love. Let it rather be like a moving sea between the shores of your souls. And stand together, and yet not too near together. For even the pillars of the temple must stand apart; and the oak tree and the cypress will not grow in each other's shadow. Remember that love gives nothing but from itself. Love possesses not, nor would it be possessed, for love is sufficient unto love. And think not that you can direct the course of love. For love, if it finds you worthy, will direct your course.

FROM *The Prophet*

KAHLIL GIBRAN

(1883–1931), Lebanese-American author

The marriage of true minds

Let me not to the marriage of true minds

Admit impediments. Love is not love

Which alters when it alteration finds,

Or bends with the remover to remove:

O no! it is an ever-fixed mark

That looks on tempests and is never shaken;

It is the star to every wandering bark,

Whose worth's unknown, although his height be taken.

Love's not Time's fool, though rosy lips and cheeks

Within his bending sickle's compass come:

Love alters not with his brief hours and weeks,

But bears it out even to the edge of doom.

If this be error and upon me proved,

I never writ, nor no man ever loved.

SONNET 116

WILLIAM SHAKESPEARE

(1564-1616), English playwright and poet

Many Waters Cannot Quench Love

She:

Your love is more fragrant than wine,
fragrant is the scent of your perfume,
and your name like perfume poured out;
for this the maidens love you.

He:

Wear me as a seal upon your heart,
as a seal upon your arm;
for love is strong as death,
passion cruel as the grave;
it blazes up like blazing fire,
fiercer than any flame.
Many waters cannot quench love,
no flood can sweep it away;
if a man were to offer for love
the whole wealth of his house,
it would be utterly scorned.
to regard this world as invisible,
and to disregard what appears to be the self.

The more we love

The love of God, Unutterable and perfect, flows into a pure soul the way light rushes into a transparent object. The more love we receive, the more love we shine forth; so that, as we grow clear and open, the more complete the joy of loving is. And the more souls who resonate together, the greater the intensity of their love for, mirror like, each soul reflects the other.

FROM *The Inferno*
DANTE ALIGHIERI
(1265–1321), Italian poet

What greater thing

What greater thing is there for two human souls than to feel that they are joined for life—to strengthen each other in all labour, to rest on each other in all sorrow, to minister to each other in all pain, to be one with each other in silent unspeakable memories at the moment of the last parting?

FROM *Adam Bede*

GEORGE ELIOT

(1819-1880), English writer

Love is something you and I must have

Love is something you and I must have. We must have it because our spirit feeds upon it. We must have it because without it we become weak and faint. Without love our self esteem weakens. Without it our courage fails. Without love we can no longer look out confidently at the world. Instead we turn inwardly and begin to feed upon our own personalities and little by little we destroy ourselves.

FROM *My Heart Soars*

CHIEF DAN GEORGE

(1899–1981), Salish Band, British Columbia

Love feels no burden

Love feels no burden, regards not labors, strives toward more than it attains, argues not of impossibility, since it believes that it may and can do all things. Therefore it avails for all things, and fulfills and accomplishes much where one not a lover falls and lies helpless.

FROM *The Imitation of Christ*

THOMAS À KEMPIS

(1380–1471), German priest and writer

My Delight and Thy Delight

My delight and thy delight
Walking, like two angels white,
In the gardens of the night:

My desire and thy desire
Twining to a tongue of fire,
Leaping live, and laughing higher:

Thro' the everlasting strife
In the mysteries of life.
Love, from whom the world begun,
Hath the secret of the sun.

Love can tell, and love alone,
Whence the million stars were
    strewn.

This he taught us, this we knew,
Happy in his science true,
Hand in hand as we stood
'Neath the shadows of the wood,
Heart to heart as we lay
In the dawning of the day.

Why each atom knows its own,
How, in spite of woe and death,
Gay is life, and sweet is breath:

How do I love thee?

How do I love thee? Let me count the ways.
I love thee to the depth and breadth and height
My soul can reach, when feeling out of sight
For the ends of being and ideal grace.
I love thee to the level of every day's
Most quiet need, by sun and candle-light.
I love thee freely, as men strive for right.
I love thee purely, as they turn from praise.
I love thee with the passion put to use
In my old griefs, and with my childhood's faith.
I love thee with a love I seemed to lose
With my lost saints. I love thee with the breath,
Smiles, tears, of all my life; and, if God choose,
I shall but love thee better after death.

ELIZABETH BARRETT BROWNING

(1806–1861), English Romantic poet

Love courses
through everything

Love courses through everything,

No, Love is everything.

How can you say, there is no love,

when nothing but Love exists?

All that you see has appeared because of Love.

All shines from Love,

All pulses with Love,

All flows from Love—

No, once again all is Love!

FAKHRUDDIN ARAQI

(1213–1289), Sufi mystic

Love is a portion
of the soul itself

Love is a portion of the soul itself,
and it is of the same nature as the
celestial breathing of the atmosphere of paradise.

VICTOR HUGO

(1802–1885), French Romantic poet and dramatist

Wild Nights!

Wild Nights! Wild Nights! were I with thee

Wild Nights would be our luxury.

Futile the winds to a heart in port, Gone with the compass

Gone with the chart–Rowing in Eden.

Ah the Sea! Might I but moor–Tonight in thee.

Time is too slow

Time is too slow for those who wait,

too swift for those who fear,

too long for those who grieve,

too short for those who rejoice, but for those who love,

time is eternity.

This is Love

This is love: to fly toward a secret sky,
to cause a hundred veils to fall each moment.
First, to let go of life.
In the end, to take a step without feet;
to regard this world as invisible,
and to disregard what appears to be the self.

Heart, I said, what a gift it has been
to enter this circle of lovers,
to see beyond seeing itself,
to reach and feel within the breast.

Love Song

How can I keep my soul in me, so that it doesn't touch your soul?

How can I raise it high enough, past you, to other things?

I would like to shelter it, among remote lost objects,

in some dark and silent place that doesn't resonate

when your depths resound.

Yet everything that touches us, me and you,

takes us together like a violin's bow,

which draws one voice out of two separate strings.

Upon what instrument are we two spanned?

And what musician holds us in his hand?

Oh sweetest song.

RAINER MARIA RILKE
(1875-1926), German lyric poet

William Henry Ruse

OF THE 97TH OHIO VOLUNTEER REGIMENT TO

Maggie Stewart

&

OF ADAMSVILLE, OHIO

during the American Civil War (1861–1865)

For let me say that your memory is ever dear to me and if we never again meet on Earth I shall ever Cherish the fond remembrance of Thee, and think of the pleasant hours passed in your society, but let me indulge the hope that we may again meet ere long.

Infinite Love

Infinite Love is a weapon of matchless potency.

It is the "summum bonum" of Life.

It is an attribute of the brave, in fact it is their all.

It does not come within the reach of the coward.

It is no wooden or lifeless dogma but a living and life-giving force.

It is the special attribute of the heart.

MAHATMA GANDHI
(1869–1948), Indian spiritual and political leader

I Shall Love You

Sensual pleasure passes and vanishes in the twinkling of an eye, but the friendship between us, the mutual confidence, the delights of the heart, the enchantment of the soul, these things do not perish and can never be destroyed. I shall love you until I die.

FRANÇOIS-MARIE VOLTAIRE
(1694-1778), French Enlightenment writer

The Wedding Night

Johann Wolfgang von Goethe

Within the chamber, far away

From the glad feast, sits Love in dread
Lest guests disturb, in wanton play,

The silence of the bridal bed.
His torch's pale flame serves to gild

The scene with mystic sacred glow;
The room with incense-clouds is fill'd,

That ye may perfect rapture know.

How beats thy heart, when thou dost hear
The chime that warns thy guests to fly!
How glow'st thou for those lips so dear,

That soon are mute, and naught deny!
With her into the holy place

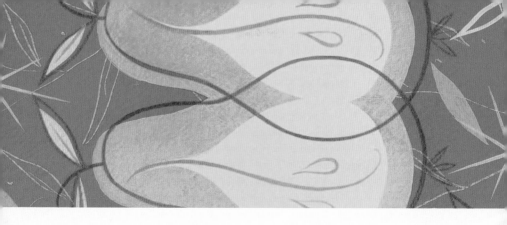

Thou hast'nest then, to perfect all;
The fire the warder's hands embrace,

Grows, like a night-light, dim and small.

How heaves her bosom, and how burns

Her face at every fervent kiss!
Her coldness now to trembling turns,

Thy daring now a duty is.
Love helps thee to undress her fast,

But thou art twice as fast as he;
And then he shuts both eye at last,

With sly and roguish modesty.

(1749–1832)
German writer and natural philosopher

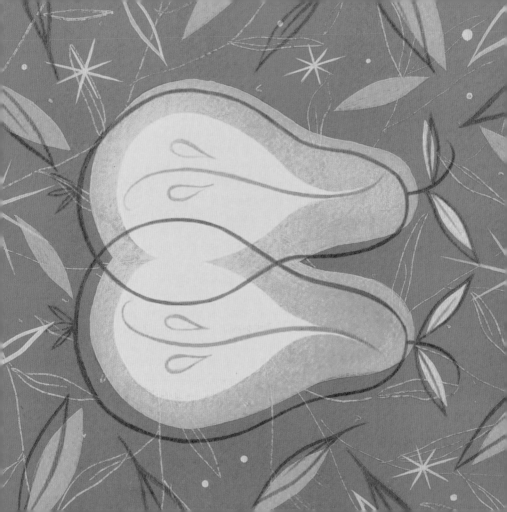